DICTIONARY OF

ENGLISH

SYNONYMS

VOCABULARY

BUILDING

MANIK JOSHI

<u>Dedication</u>

THIS BOOK IS

DEDICATED

TO THOSE

WHO REALIZE

THE POWER OF ENGLISH

AND WANT TO

LEARN IT

SINCERELY

****

<u>IMPORTANT</u> <u>NOTE</u>

This Book is Part of a Series
SERIES Name: "English Word Power"
[A Thirty-Book Series]
BOOK Number: 01
BOOK Title: "Dictionary of English Synonyms"

****

Table of Contents

DICTIONARY OF ENGLISH SYNONYMS 1

Dedication 2

Copyright Notice 3

What are "Synonyms"? 5

English Synonyms -- A 6

English Synonyms -- B 13

English Synonyms -- C 17

English Synonyms -- D 24

English Synonyms -- E 31

English Synonyms -- F...36

English Synonyms -- G 41

English Synonyms -- H 44

English Synonyms -- I..47

English Synonyms -- J 51

English Synonyms -- K 53

English Synonyms -- L...54

English Synonyms -- M..58

English Synonyms -- N 63

English Synonyms -- O 65

English Synonyms -- P 67

English Synonyms -- Q 73

English Synonyms -- R 74

English Synonyms -- S 79

English Synonyms -- T...87

English Synonyms -- U 90

English Synonyms -- V 93

English Synonyms -- W 94

English Synonyms -- XYZ...96

About the Author...97

BIBLIOGRAPHY...98

What are "Synonyms"?

Definition of Synonym:

A synonym is a word that has the same or nearly the same meaning as another word.

A synonym is the opposite of an antonym.

Synonyms-related important terms

Metonyms

Synonyms are also known as **metonyms.**

Synonymous

Words that are synonyms are said to be **synonymous.**

Synonymy

The state of being a synonym is called **synonymy.**

Important Note:

Synonymous words should belong to the same parts of speech.

Verb --

Synonyms for 'say' -- speak, tell, utter

Noun --

Synonyms for 'house' -- abode, dwelling, home, residence

Adjective --

Synonyms for 'hard' -- rigid, solid, stiff

Adverb --

Synonyms for 'attentively' -- carefully, caringly, cautiously, vigilantly, thoughtfully

English Synonyms -- A

001. ABET -- (meaning) to encourage somebody to do something illegal

Synonyms for 'Abet' --

incite / instigate / provoke

******

002. ABEYANCE -- (meaning) being stopped for a period of time

Synonyms for 'Abeyance' --

dormancy / intermission / suspension

******

003. ABILITY -- (meaning) the fact that somebody is able to do something

Synonyms for 'Ability' --

aptitude / capability / competence / knack / potential / proficiency / skill / talent

******

004. ABLAZE -- (meaning) burning; on fire

Synonyms for 'Ablaze' --

aflame / afire / alight

******

005. ABRASIVE -- (meaning) not smooth

Synonyms for 'Abrasive' --

coarse / harsh / rough

******

006. ABSENCE -- (meaning) not available, present, etc.

Synonyms for 'Absence' --

nonexistence / nonappearance / nonattendance

******

007. ABSTRUSE -- (meaning) difficult to understand

Synonyms for 'Abstruse' --

arcane / complicated / convoluted / esoteric / garbled / inarticulate / incoherent / incomprehensible / indecipherable / inexplicable / intricate / obscure / rarefied / recondite / unfathomable / unintelligible / unplumbed

******

008. ABUSE -- (meaning) unfair or cruel treatment

Synonyms for 'Abuse' --

brutality / cruelty / exploitation / ill-treatment / maltreatment / mistreatment / misuse / spitefulness / viciousness

******

009. ABYSS -- (meaning) a very deep crack in the ground

Synonyms for 'Abyss' --

chasm / gulf

******

010. ACCEDE -- (meaning) to agree to a demand, request, proposal, etc.

Synonyms for 'Accede' --

acquiesce / approve / assent / commend / comply / endorse / grant / permission / ratify / sanction

******

011. ACCENTUATE -- (meaning) to make something more noticeable

Synonyms for 'Accentuate' --

emphasize / highlight / underline / underscore

******

012. ACCLIMATIZE -- (meaning) to get used to a new situation

Synonyms for 'Acclimatize' --

adapt / adjust

******

013. ACCOMPLISH -- (meaning) to succeed in getting something

Synonyms for 'Accomplish' --

attain / conquer / manage

******

014. ACCOST -- (meaning) to come near to somebody/something

Synonyms for 'Accost' --

advance / approach / confront

******

015. ACCREDITED -- (meaning) officially recognized

Synonyms for 'Accredited' --

certified / endorsed / licensed

******

016. ACCRUAL -- (meaning) increase in something over a period of time

Synonyms for 'Accrual' --

accretion / addition / amassing / buildup / gathering

******

017. ACCUSE -- (meaning) to say somebody is guilty of something

Synonyms for 'Accuse' --

arraign / blame / charge / impeach / indict / prosecute

******

018. ACQUIT -- (meaning) to say officially that somebody is not guilty of a crime

Synonyms for 'Acquit' --

absolve / exculpate / exonerate

******

019. ADMIRATION -- (meaning) praise or approval

Synonyms for 'Admiration' --

acclaim / accolade / applause / approbation / commendation / ovation

******

020. ADMIRING -- (meaning) behavior that shows that you respect somebody/something

Synonyms for 'Admiring' --

chivalrous / considerate / courteous / deferential / gracious / respectful / reverent / reverential

******

021. ADROIT -- (meaning) skillful and accurate

Synonyms for 'Adroit' --

agile / deft / dexterous / natty / nifty / nimble / swift

******

022. ALARMING -- (meaning) causing feeling of fear and worry

Synonyms for 'Alarming' --

baffling / bewildering / confounding / disconcerting / disquieting / distressing / perplexing / puzzling / tormenting / upsetting / worrying

******

023. ALIKE -- (meaning) like someone or something else

Synonyms for 'Alike' --

analogous / same / similar

******

024. ALLEVIATE -- (meaning) to make something less unpleasant

Synonyms for 'Alleviate' --

assuage / ease / mitigate

******

025. AMBIANCE -- (meaning) the feeling that somebody has in a particular place or situation

Synonyms for **'Ambiance'** --

atmosphere / environment / mood / surroundings / vibes

******

026. AMPLE -- (meaning) more than enough

Synonyms for **'Ample'** --

abundance / cornucopia / plenty / plethora / profusion

******

027. ANNOY -- (meaning) to make somebody uncomfortable or angry by asking for something, or asking to do something, or doing or saying unpleasant things

Synonyms for **'Annoy'** --

badger / beleaguer / bother / exasperate / harass / infuriate / irritate / pester / plague

******

028. APPARITION -- (meaning) soul of a dead person

Synonyms for **'Apparition'** --

ghost / ghoul / phantom / poltergeist / specter / spirit

******

029. APPREHEND -- (meaning) to capture somebody/something

Synonyms for **'Apprehend'** --

arrest / detain / grab / seize

******

030. APPROVE -- (meaning) to officially agree to a plan, etc.

Synonyms for **'Approve'** --

assent / consent / pass / sanction

******

031. APPROXIMATELY -- (meaning) more or less accurate

Synonyms for 'Approximately' --

almost / around / nearly / roughly

******

032. ARGUE -- (meaning) disagreeing angrily in conversation

Synonyms for 'Argue' --

bicker / debate / joust / quarrel / row / spar / squabble / wrangle

******

033. ASSIST -- (meaning) to help somebody

Synonyms for 'Assist' --

aid / cooperate / facilitate / support

******

034. ASSOCIATION -- (meaning) a group of people who have joined together with a official purpose

Synonyms for 'Association' --

alliance / coalition / confederation / federation / league / organization / union

******

035. ATROCIOUS -- (meaning) very bad, cruel, shocking or unpleasant

Synonyms for 'Atrocious' --

abysmal / appalling / awful / contemptible / dreadful / fearful / fearsome / frightening / frightful / horrible / terrible / terrifying / vile

******

036. ATTIRE – fine or formal clothes

Synonyms for 'Attire' --

apparel / clothing / costume / dress / garb / gear / outfit / uniform

******

037. AUSPICIOUS -- (meaning) likely to produce a successful result

Synonyms for **'Auspicious'** --

blessed / fortunate / lucky / promising / propitious

******

038. AWKWARDNESS -- (meaning) moving or doing things in a strange way

Synonyms for **'Awkwardness'** --

clumsiness / coarseness / crudeness / discomfiture / gaucheness / gawkiness / gracelessness / inelegance / ineptness / klutziness / nervousness / tackiness / tactlessness / uncouthness / ungainliness / unseemliness / unwieldiness

******

English Synonyms -- B

039. BABBLE -- (meaning) to talk nonsense

*Synonyms for **'Babble'** --*

blabber / blather / burble / chatter / drivel / gabble / gibber / jabber / jaw / natter / prate / prattle / rant

******

040. BABYISH -- (meaning) typical of a baby; immature

*Synonyms for **'Babyish'** --*

childish / infantile / juvenile / puerile

******

041. BACKLASH -- (meaning) strong reaction towards an action or event

*Synonyms for **'Backlash'** --*

aftermath / counterattack / repercussion

******

042. BAD-TEMPERED -- (meaning) in an angry mood

*Synonyms for **'Bad-tempered'** --*

argumentative / cantankerous / confrontational / crabby / irritable / quarrelsome / tetchy

******

043. BARBARIC -- (meaning) having a desire to cause pain and suffering; cruel, harsh, unkind

*Synonyms for **'Barbaric'** --*

atrocious / bestial / boorish / brutal / brutish / callous / cold-blooded / coldhearted / compassionless / ferocious / hardhearted / hardnosed / heartless / inhuman / insensitive / merciless / pitiless / ruthless / savage / thoughtless / unfeeling / unforgiving / unsympathetic

******

044. BARGAIN -- (meaning) to reach an agreement, especially about the price of something

*Synonyms for **'Bargain'** --*

deal / haggle / negotiate / settle

******

045. BARREN -- (meaning) unable to produce good crops

*Synonyms for **'Barren'** --*

infertile / sterile / uncultivable / unproductive

******

046. BATTER -- (meaning) to hit somebody/something hard

*Synonyms for **'Batter'** --*

bash / beat / clobber / clout / cuff / hammer / knock / pound / pummel / punch / rap / slap / smack / sock / spank / strike / thrash / thump / thwack / wallop / whack

******

047. BATTY -- (meaning) slightly crazy

*Synonyms for **'Batty'** --*

nutty / wacky / weird

******

048. BEHIND -- (meaning) towards the back

*Synonyms for **'Behind'** --*

backward / rearward

******

049. BEND -- (meaning) to tilt or make something tilt; to change direction of something

*Synonyms for **'Bend'** --*

angle / bow / coil / crook / curl / curve / deviate / distort / duck / lean / loop / mold / slant / slope / swerve / turn / twine / twirl / twist / warp / weave / wind

******

050. BETRAYAL -- (meaning) not being loyal to somebody who trusts you; deceit

Synonyms for **'Betrayal'** --

disloyalty / **infidelity** / **perfidy** / **treachery** / **treason**

******

051. BIGOT -- (meaning) a person having strong, unreasonable beliefs

Synonyms for **'Bigot'** --

chauvinist / **dogmatist** / **extremist** / **fanatic** / **racist** / **radical**

******

052. BLISTERING -- (meaning) extremely hot

Synonyms for **'Blistering'** --

baking / **blazing** / **boiling** / **burning** / **flaming** / **frying** / **roasting** / **scorching** / **searing** / **sizzling** / **smoldering** / **steaming** / **sweltering**

******

053. BOOST -- (meaning) to become something better, stronger or more successful; to increase something

Synonyms for **'Boost'** --

advance / **augment** / **bolster** / **boost** / **buttress** / **embolden** / **heighten** / **reinforce** / **strengthen** / **vitalize**

******

054. BOSS -- (meaning) in charge of an organization

Synonyms for **'Boss'** --

chief / **director** / **executive** / **head** / **manager** / **supervisor**

******

055. BOTTOM -- (meaning) the lowest part of something

Synonyms for 'Bottom' --

base / floor / foundation

******

056. BRAWNY -- (meaning) having strong, solid body

Synonyms for 'Brawny' --

beefy / burly / chunky / hefty / muscular / robust / stocky / stout / strapping / sturdy / thickset

******

057. BRIMFUL -- (meaning) full of something

Synonyms for 'Brimful' --

crammed / heaving / laden / loaded / packed / teeming

******

058. BUFFET -- (meaning) to push somebody/something roughly

Synonyms for 'Buffet' --

knock / pummel / stroke

******

059. BURST -- (meaning) to damage something forcefully

Synonyms for 'Burst' --

fracture / rupture / shatter / splinter / split

******

060. BYZANTINE ---- difficult to change or understand

Synonyms for 'Byzantine' --

complex / complicated / convoluted / intricate / knotty

******

English Synonyms -- C

061. CALLOW -- (meaning) young and inexperienced

Synonyms for 'Callow' --

ham-fisted / immature / incompetent / inept / naïve / unprofessional

******

062. CANDIDLY -- (meaning) directly

Synonyms for 'Candidly' --

blatantly / explicitly / overtly / plainly

******

063. CATASTROPHE -- (meaning) a sudden event causing heavy damage

Synonyms for 'Catastrophe' --

calamity / cataclysm / devastation / disaster

******

064. CELEBRATED -- (meaning) famous and respected

Synonyms for 'Celebrated' --

distinguished / eminent / extraordinary / legendary / notable / noteworthy / outstanding / prominent / remarkable / renowned

******

065. CHAOS -- situation of no order or control

Synonyms for 'Chaos' --

bedlam / commotion / disarray / disorder / havoc / lawlessness / mayhem / pandemonium / racket / tumult / turmoil / uproar

******

066. CHARACTERISTIC -- (meaning) a typical quality of something

Synonyms for 'Characteristic' --

attribute / feature / peculiarity / trait

******

067. CHEERFULNESS -- (meaning) feeling of happiness

Synonyms for 'Cheerfulness' --

briskness / conviviality / ebullience / gaiety / glee / hilarity / jauntiness / jolliness / jollity / joviality / joyfulness / jubilation / merriment / mirth / spryness

******

068. CHERISHED -- (meaning) very valuable

Synonyms for 'Cherished' --

esteemed / prized / treasured

******

069. CHOOSE -- (meaning) to make a choice

Synonyms for 'Choose' --

decide / opt / pick / select

******

070. CHUBBY -- (meaning) slightly fat and attractive

Synonyms for 'Chubby' --

corpulent / flabby / fleshy / podgy / plump / rotund / stout / tubby

******

071. CHUCK -- (meaning) to throw something in a careless way

Synonyms for 'Chuck' --

fling / hurl / lob / pitch / sling / toss

******

072. CHUNK -- (meaning) large piece of something like food, etc.

Synonyms for 'Chunk' --

hunk / lump / portion

******

073. CIRCUMSTANCE -- (meaning) particular conditions and facts about an action or event
Synonyms for 'Circumstance' --
status / position / situation

******

074. CITE -- (meaning) to provide facts, reasons, etc. to prove your point
Synonyms for 'Cite' --
adduce / mention / quote

******

075. CLASSIFICATION -- (meaning) the act of putting things, etc. into groups
Synonyms for 'Classification' --
categorization / grouping / itemization / cataloging / sorting

******

076. COLLOQUY -- (meaning) an informal talk that involves two people or a small group of people
Synonyms for 'Colloquy' --
banter / chat / conversation / dialogue / parley

******

077. COMBINE -- (meaning) to bring two or more things together to form a single one
Synonyms for 'Combine' --
blend / connect / join / merge / mingle / unite

******

078. COMFY -- (meaning) comfortable and safe
Synonyms for 'Comfy' --
cozy / homely / snug

******

079. COMMENCE -- (meaning) to begin or start something

Synonyms for ***'Commence'*** --

activate / **create** / **inaugurate** / **initiate** / **instigate** / **institute** / **introduce** / **launch** / **originate**

******

080. COMMENSURATE -- (meaning) similar to something in amount, significance, quality, etc.

Synonyms for ***'Commensurate'*** --

appropriate / **matching** / **corresponding** / **proportionate**

******

081. COMPACT -- (meaning) to make something more firm, strong, dense, etc.

Synonyms for ***'Compact'*** --

compress / **condense** / **concentrate**

******

082. CONCEAL -- (meaning) to cover somebody/something completely

Synonyms for ***'Conceal'*** --

blanket / **camouflage** / **cloak** / **disguise** / **enfold** / **envelop** / **hide** / **mantle** / **mask** / **plaster** / **shroud** / **veil** / **wrap**

******

083. CONFUSE -- (meaning) to make somebody unable to think clearly

Synonyms for ***'Confuse'*** --

addle / **baffle** / **bamboozle** / **befog** / **bewilder** / **confound** / **muddle** / **mystify** / **perplex** / **puzzle**

******

084. CONFUSING -- (meaning) not clear

Synonyms for 'Confusing' --

ambiguous / **baffling** / **bamboozling** / **bewildering** / **confounding** / **muddling** / **mystifying** / **perplexing** / **puzzling** / **vague**

******

085. CONSCIOUS -- (meaning) noticing something

Synonyms for 'Conscious' --

alert / **aware** / **cognizant** / **mindful**

******

086. CONSIDER -- (meaning) to think about something carefully

Synonyms for 'Consider' --

cogitate / **contemplate** / **judge** / **muse** / **ponder** / **ruminate**

******

087. CONSTANTLY -- (meaning) at all times

Synonyms for 'Constantly' --

always / **continually** / **recurrently** / **repetitively**

******

088. CONSTRAINED -- (meaning) controlled by rules, laws, etc.

Synonyms for 'Constrained' --

curbed / **limited** / **restrained** / **restricted**

******

089. CONSUL -- (meaning) a high ranking government officer who represents his/her country in a foreign country

Synonyms for 'Consul' --

ambassador / **diplomat** / **emissary** / **envoy**

******

090. CONTRACTION -- (meaning) to become gradually narrower

Synonyms for 'Contraction' --

lessening / narrowing / tapering

******

091. CONVALESCE -- (meaning) to get back your health

Synonyms for 'Convalesce' --

heal / recuperate / recover

******

092. CONVENIENT -- (meaning) very useful

Synonyms for 'Convenient' --

apposite / handy / fitting / suitable

******

093. CONVERT -- (meaning) to change something

Synonyms for 'Convert' --

amend / modify / transform

******

094. CORDIAL -- (meaning) friendly and pleasant

Synonyms for 'Cordial' --

gracious / hospitable / welcoming

******

095. CORE -- (meaning) the central part of something

Synonyms for 'Core' --

axis / focus / hub / middle / nucleus

******

096. CRAFTINESS -- (meaning) the fact of being clever

Synonyms for 'Craftiness' --

astuteness / conniving / cunning / deceit / devious / manipulative / scheming / shrewdness / slyness / sneakiness / wily

******

097. CRAVE -- (meaning) to want something very much

Synonyms for 'Crave' --

aim / aspire / covet / desire / hanker / intend / long / seek / wish / yearn

******

098. CREATIVITY -- (meaning) ability to produce something new

Synonyms for 'Creativity' --

imaginativeness / ingenuity / inventiveness / originality

******

099. CROOKED -- (meaning) not straight

Synonyms for 'Crooked' --

arched / bent / bowed / curled / curved / hooked / twisted / warped

******

100. CUT -- (meaning) to make an opening using sharp tool

Synonyms for 'Cut' --

carve / chop / gash / grate / hack / hew / lacerate / mince / rip / scythe / sever / shred / slash / slice / slit / whittle

******

English Synonyms -- D

101. DAINTILY -- (meaning) attractively or carefully

*Synonyms for **'Daintily'** --*

delicately / **elegantly** / **exquisitely** / **gracefully** / **sophisticatedly** / **stylishly**

******

102. DALLY -- (meaning) to do something too slowly

*Synonyms for **'Dally'** --*

dawdle / **delay** / **linger** / **loiter** / **lurk**

******

103. DANGLE -- (meaning) to hang or swing freely

*Synonyms for **'Dangle'** --*

bow / **droop** / **hang** / **sag** / **suspend** / **sway** / **swing** / **wilt**

******

104. DAPPLED -- (meaning) marked with spots or patches of color or shade

*Synonyms for **'Dappled'** --*

blotchy / **dotted** / **freckled** / **marked** / **mottled** / **patterned** / **piebald** / **pockmarked** / **speckled** / **spotty** / **sprinkled** / **stippled**

******

105. DASTARDLY -- (meaning) evil and cruel

*Synonyms for **'Dastardly'** --*

appalling / **deplorable** / **depraved** / **detestable** / **dishonorable** / **ignoble** / **ignominious** / **impious** / **reprehensible** / **sinful** / **wicked**

******

106. DAUB -- (meaning) to carelessly spread a thick or sticky substance onto something

Synonyms for 'Daub' --

smear / smudge / spatter / splash / splatter

******

107. DAYBREAK -- (meaning) the time of day when sunlight first appears

Synonyms for 'Daybreak' --

dawn / morning / sunrise / sunup

******

108. DECAY -- (meaning) to be destroyed gradually

Synonyms for 'Decay' --

decompose / perish / putrefy / rot

******

109. DECEPTION -- (meaning) the act of making somebody believe something that is false

Synonyms for 'Deception' --

charade / con / fake / fraud / hoax / ruse / sham / swindle / travesty / trick

******

110. DECORATE -- (meaning) to make something look more attractive

Synonyms for 'Decorate' --

adorn / beautify / bedeck / bejewel / embellish / emboss / embroider / festoon / garnish / modernize / ornament / prettify / refurbish / renovate / revamp / titivate

******

111. DEFECT -- (meaning) a mistake, error or weakness

Synonyms for 'Defect' --

blemish / flaw / fault / shortcoming

******

112. DEGRADE -- (meaning) showing you have no respect for somebody

*Synonyms for **'Degrade'** --*

abase / belittle / debase / demean / deride / disparage / humiliate

******

113. DELUSION -- (meaning) an idea based on incorrect information

*Synonyms for **'Delusion'** --*

fallacy / misapprehension / misconception / misconstruction / misinterpretation / misreading / misunderstanding

******

114. DELIBERATE -- (meaning) planned in advance

*Synonyms for **'Deliberate'** --*

intended / intentional / premeditated / purposeful

******

115. DELIGHTFUL -- (meaning) very pleasant

*Synonyms for **'Delightful'** --*

alluring / appealing / charismatic / charming / enchanting

******

116. DEPRESSING -- (meaning) making you very sad; without hope

*Synonyms for **'Depressing'** --*

bleak / dejected / demoralizing / despondent / disappointing / gloomy / hapless / miserable / wretched

******

117. DESPERATE -- (meaning) without any hope

*Synonyms for **'Desperate'** --*

abject / dejected / depressing / disconsolate / discouraging / dismal / forlorn / heartbroken / miserable / pitiful / unpromising / wretched

******

118. DEMANDING -- (meaning) extensive mental or physical effort

Synonyms for 'Demanding' --

arduous / challenging / draining / exhausting / grueling / laborious / onerous / painstaking / strenuous / taxing / tiring / tough

******

119. DESIST -- (meaning) to stop doing something, especially something you want to do

Synonyms for 'Desist' --

abstain / refrain / relinquish / renounce

******

120. DETEST -- (meaning) to hate something very much

Synonyms for 'Detest' --

abhor / abominate / despise / loathe / nauseate / scorn

******

121. DETERMINED -- (meaning) having made firm decision; not changing

Synonyms for 'Determined' --

adamant / feisty / gritty / resolute / staunch / steadfast / strong-minded / unwavering

Note: The following words are used to show 'DETERMINATION in an unreasonable way' (Disapproving).

defiant / dogmatic / headstrong / inflexible / mulish / obdurate / obstinate / pigheaded / rigid / stubborn / unbending

******

122. DEVIANT -- (meaning) something that is not normal or acceptable

Synonyms for 'Deviant' --

aberrant / anomalous / unusual

******

123. DICTIONARY -- (meaning) a book that comprises an alphabetical list of words and their meanings

Synonyms for **'Dictionary'** --

glossary / lexicon / terminology / thesaurus / vocabulary

******

124. DIMINISH -- (meaning) to become lesser

Synonyms for **'Diminish'** --

dwindle / drop / lessen / reduce

******

125. DISCORD -- (meaning) not in agreement

Synonyms for **'Discord'** --

conflict / disagreement / dispute / dissension / dissent / dissonance / opposition

******

126. DISENGAGE -- (meaning) to free somebody/something from somebody/something that is holding it

Synonyms for **'Disengage'** --

detach / disentangle / release / unbolt / unbutton / unchain / unfasten / unhook / unknot / unleash / unlock / unpack / unravel / unscrew / unshackle / untangle / unwrap / unyoke

******

127. DISGRACE -- (meaning) loss of respect

Synonyms for **'Disgrace'** --

discredit / dishonor / humiliation / ignominy / shame

******

128. DISGUSTING -- (meaning) extremely unpleasant

Synonyms for 'Disgusting' --

abhorrent / abominable / despicable / detestable / hideous / horrid / loathsome / nasty / nauseating / obnoxious / repugnant / repulsive / revolting / unsightly / vile

******

129. DISOWN -- (meaning) to leave or lose something

Synonyms for 'Disown' --

abandon / cede / concede / desert / discard / discontinue / dump / forfeit / forgo / forsake / quit / recant / relinquish / renounce / surrender / withdraw / yield

******

130. DISPERSE -- (meaning) to move in different directions

Synonyms for 'Disperse' --
scatter / spread / swell

******

131. DISPLACE -- (meaning) to remove somebody/something from its position or place

Synonyms for 'Displace' --
dislocate / disjoint / dislodge

******

132. DISRUPTIVE -- (meaning) to interrupt an activity, process, etc. by causing problems

Synonyms for 'Disruptive' --
disorderly / disrupting / troublemaking / troublesome / troubling / unruly / wild

******

133. DODGE -- (meaning) to cleverly stay away from somebody/something
Synonyms for 'Dodge' --

avoid / **elude** / **evade**

******

134. DREARY -- (meaning) dull and not exciting

Synonyms for **'Dreary'** --

boring / **droning** / **lackluster** / **miserable** / **monotonous** / **tedious** / **unexciting** / **uninteresting** / **wearisome** / **wearying**

******

135. DULCET -- (meaning) sounding sweet and pleasant

Synonyms for **'Dulcet'** --

mellifluous / **melodious** / **musical** / **tuneful**

******

English Synonyms -- E

136. EAGER -- (meaning) extremely interested in something

Synonyms for 'Eager' --

agitated / animated / ardent / energized / enthusiastic / excited / fervent / impatient / impetuous / passionate / thrilled / willing / zealous

******

137. EARMARK -- (meaning) to keep something for a particular purpose

Synonyms for 'Earmark' --

allocate / allot / assign / reserve

******

138. EARNEST– (meaning) genuine and honest

Synonyms for 'Earnest' --

sincere / solemn / wholehearted

******

139. ECHELON -- (meaning) a position of authority in an organization

Synonyms for 'Echelon' --

band / grade / level / rank / stratum

******

140. ECONOMIC -- (meaning) connected with money and finance

Synonyms for 'Economic' --

financial / fiscal / monetary / pecuniary

******

141. ECSTASY -- (meaning) great happiness

Synonyms for 'Ecstasy' --

bliss / delight / euphoria / exultation / jubilation

******

142. EDGE -- (meaning) the outside limit of an object, etc.

Synonyms for 'Edge' --

border / boundary / rim

******

143. EDICT -- (meaning) an official order

Synonyms for 'Edict' --

command / decree / diktat / law / proclamation / ruling / statute / verdict

******

144. ELIMINATE -- (meaning) to get rid of something

Synonyms for 'Eliminate' --

annihilate / decimate / eradicate / exterminate / obliterate / purge

******

145. ELLIPSIS -- (meaning) short form

Synonyms for 'Ellipsis' --

abbreviation / acronym / contraction

******

146. EMBARRASS -- (meaning) making somebody ashamed

Synonyms for 'Embarrass' --

abash / debase / discomfit / disgrace / dishonor / humiliate / mortify

******

147. ENACT -- (meaning) to make something legally valid

Synonyms for 'Enact' --

approve / authorize / empower / endorse / sanction

******

148. ENORMOUS -- (meaning) extremely large, big or great

Synonyms for 'Enormous' --

colossal / cosmic / expansive / extensive / gargantuan / gigantic / grand / huge / immense / mammoth / massive / monumental / titanic / vast / widespread

******

149. ENRAGE -- (meaning) to make somebody very angry

Synonyms for 'Enrage' --

aggrieve / annoy / exasperate / goad / incense / infuriate / irate / irritate / livid / madden / peeve / pique / rankle / rile

******

150. ENTHUSIASM -- (meaning) strong feeling of excitement and interest

Synonyms for 'Enthusiasm' --

alacrity / bravura / eagerness / fervor / gusto / keenness / passion / zeal / zest

******

151. ENTICE -- (meaning) to trick somebody to do something by offering a reward

Synonyms for 'Entice' --

lure / seduce / tempt

******

152. ERATICALLY -- (meaning) happening irregularly [at irregular times or in irregular ways]

Synonyms for 'Eratically' --

disconnectedly / fitfully / inconsistently / indiscriminately / intermittently / occasionally / patchily / randomly / sporadically / unevenly / unsteadily / variably

******

153. ESCORT -- (meaning) to go or travel somewhere with somebody

Synonyms for 'Escort' --

accompany / convoy / usher

******

154. EVALUATE -- (meaning) to make a judgment about value or quality

Synonyms for 'Evaluate' --

appraise / assess / judge

******

155. EXACERBATE -- (meaning) to become worse

Synonyms for 'Exacerbate' --

aggravate / deteriorate / worsen

******

156. EXCITING -- (meaning) causing great interest

Synonyms for 'Exciting' --

absorbing / awe-inspiring / breathtaking / captivating / compelling / elating / electrifying / engrossing / enlivening / entrancing / exhilarating / fascinating / gripping / inspiring / intriguing / mesmerizing / riveting / rousing / spellbinding / stimulating / stirring / thrilling

******

157. EXERTION -- (meaning) hard work

Synonyms for 'Exertion' --

labor / striving / toil

******

158. EXORBITANT -- (meaning) very expensive

Synonyms for 'Exorbitant' --

costly / overpriced / unaffordable

******

159. EXPLICATE -- (meaning) to describe

Synonyms for 'Explicate' --

clarify / elaborate / elucidate / explain / expound

******

160. EXTEND -- (meaning) to make something longer or larger

Synonyms for 'Extend' --

broaden / elongate / enlarge / expand / inflate / lengthen / stretch / swell / widen

******

English Synonyms -- F

161. FAKE -- (meaning) not genuine

Synonyms for 'Fake' --

artificial / **imitation** / **synthetic**

******

162. FAMISHED -- (meaning) very hungry

Synonyms for 'Famished' --

ravenous / **starving** / **voracious**

******

163. FANTASY -- (meaning) a false idea, story, etc.

Synonyms for 'Fantasy' --

fable / **fiction** / **myth**

******

164. FAREWELL -- (meaning) the act of saying Goodbye

Synonyms for 'Farewell' --

adieu / **bye-bye** / **leave-taking** / **send-off** / **valediction**

******

165. FEAT -- (meaning) a great success

Synonyms for 'Feat' --

accomplishment / **achievement** / **deed** / **triumph**

******

166. FERVENT -- (meaning) showing very strong and sincere feelings

Synonyms for 'Fervent' --

ardent / **avid** / **eager** / **excited** / **heated** / **intense** / **keen** / **passionate** / **vehement** / **zealous**

******

167. FIGHT -- (meaning) to verbally or physically struggle with somebody

Synonyms for 'Fight' --

battle / brawl / clash / conflict / wrestle

******

168. FILCH -- (meaning) to steal something of small value

Synonyms for 'Filch' --

nick / pilfer / pinch

******

169. FINE -- (meaning) all right

Synonyms for 'Fine' --

okay / satisfactory / well

******

170. FIRMLY -- (meaning) in a very strong way

Synonyms for 'Firmly' --

absolutely / ardently / boldly / categorically / certainly / compactly / completely / confidently / consistently / courageously / daringly / decisively / definitely / determinedly / energetically / enormously / entirely / exactly / fearlessly / forcefully / heroically / impressively / incontestably / indefatigably / indisputably / indomitably / indubitably / inflexibly / insistently / irrefutably / mightily / mulishly / patiently / positively / powerfully / reliably / remarkably / resolutely / robustly / securely / solidly / stalwartly / stanchly / steadfastly / strictly / stubbornly / surely / tenaciously / tightly / tirelessly / totally / unconditionally / undeniably / unfalteringly / unquestionably / unreservedly / unshakably / unswervingly / untiringly / utterly / vigorously / wholeheartedly

******

171. FLEE -- (meaning) to leave a place secretly

*Synonyms for **'Flee'** --*

abscond / **getaway** / **escape**

******

172. FLEXIBLE -- able to bend, stretched, pulled easily without breaking

*Synonyms for **'Flexible'** --*

elastic / **expandable** / **malleable** / **pliant** / **resilient** / **springy** / **stretchy** / **supple**

******

173. FLOURISH -- (meaning) to make progress quickly

*Synonyms for **'Flourish'** --*

blossom / **grow** / **prosper** / **thrive**

******

174. FOE -- (meaning) a person who hates somebody

*Synonyms for **'Foe'** --*

adversary / **antagonist** / **enemy** / **rival**

******

175. FOLLOWING -- (meaning) happening after something else

*Synonyms for **'Following'** --*

consequent / **ensuing** / **subsequent** / **succeeding** / **latter**

******

176. FOREBODING -- (meaning) feeling that something unpleasant is going to happen

*Synonyms for **'Foreboding'** --*

ominous / **portentous** / **premonition** / **sinister**

******

177. FORMER -- (meaning) happening before something else

*Synonyms for **'Former'** --*

past / previous / preceding

******

178. FORWARDS -- (meaning) towards the front

Synonyms for 'Forwards' --

ahead / afore / onwards

******

179. FRAGRANCE -- (meaning) pleasant smell

Synonyms for 'Fragrance' --

aroma / perfume / scent

******

180. FRAIL -- (meaning) unwell

Synonyms for 'Frail' --

ailing / infirm / sick

******

181. FRANK -- (meaning) honest and direct

Synonyms for 'Frank' --

blunt / candid / straightforward

******

182. FROTH -- (meaning) mass of bubbles

Synonyms for 'Froth' --

fizz / foam / froth / lather / spume / suds

******

183. FORGIVE -- (meaning) to say that you are sorry

Synonyms for 'Forgive' --

absolve / apology / excuse / pardon / reprieve

******

184. FORTRESS -- (meaning) a building built in order to defend an area

Synonyms for 'Fortress' --

bastion / castle / citadel / fort / stronghold

******

185. FRIGID -- (meaning) extremely cold

Synonyms for 'Frigid' --

arctic / chilly / freezing / frosty / glacial / icy / nippy / wintry

******

186. FUMING -- (meaning) very angry

Synonyms for 'Fuming' --

enraged / furious / infuriated

******

187. FUNDAMENTAL -- (meaning) most necessary part of something

Synonyms for 'Fundamental' --

basic / core / elemental / elementary / essential / primary / rudimentary

******

188. FUNNY -- (meaning) making you laugh

Synonyms for 'Funny' --

amusing / comical / droll / hilarious / humorous / laughable / wacky / witty / zany

******

189. FURTIVE -- (meaning) tending to hide your ideas, feelings, etc. from other people

Synonyms for 'Furtive' --

clandestine / covert / secretive / sly / sneaky / stealthy / surreptitious / undercover

******

English Synonyms -- G

190. GAFFE -- (meaning) an embarrassing mistake

Synonyms for 'Gaffe' --

blooper / blunder / bungle / faux pas / howler

******

191. GALLANT -- (meaning) showing courage; brave

Synonyms for 'Gallant' --

audacious / bold / courageous / daring / fearless / gutsy / indomitable / intrepid / plucky / resolute / spirited / unafraid / unconquerable / undaunted / valiant

******

192. GAZE -- (meaning) to look steadily at somebody/something for a long time

Synonyms for 'Gaze' --

gape / gawk / stare

******

193. GENUINE -- (meaning) real

Synonyms for 'Genuine' --

actual / authentic / bona fide / definite / factual / indisputable / justifiable / legal / legitimate / reliable / rightful / valid / veritable

******

194. GLOBAL -- (meaning) covering the whole world

Synonyms for 'Global' --

international / universal / worldly / worldwide

******

195. GLOOMY -- (meaning) nearly dark

Synonyms for 'Gloomy' --

dim / dull / murky / overcast

******

196. GORGEOUS -- (meaning) very beautiful and attractive
Synonyms for ‘Gorgeous’ --
dazzling / **striking** / **stunning**

******

197. GRAB -- (meaning) to hold something firmly
Synonyms for ‘Grab’ --
clasp / **clench** / **clutch** / **grapple** / **grasp** / **grip**

******

198. GRACIOUS -- (meaning) showing good manners
Synonyms for ‘Gracious’ --
cultured / **courteous** / **refined**

******

199. GRIEF -- (meaning) a feeling of great sadness
Synonyms for ‘Grief’ --
distress / **mourning** / **sorrow**

******

200. GRIEVE -- (meaning) to feel great sadness
Synonyms for ‘Grieve’ --
bemoan / **bewail** / **lament** / **mourn**

******

201. GRIMACE -- (meaning) to make an ugly expression with your face
Synonyms for ‘Grimace’ --
contort / **frown** / **glower** / **glare** / **scowl** / **twist**

******

202. GRACEFUL -- (meaning) kind and polite behavior; attractive
Synonyms for ‘Graceful’ --

charming / chic / cultured / elegant / genteel / polished / smart / sophisticated / stylish

******

203. GRADE -- (meaning) a level of ability or skill
Synonyms for 'Grade' --
position / ranking / rating / review / standing / score

******

204. GROUP -- (meaning) a large number of something that is connected in some way
Synonyms for 'Group' --
army / band / barrage / batch / bevy / board / bouquet / bunch / bundle / caravan / chain / choir / class / cloud / clump / cluster / clutter / code / collection / company / crew / crowd / drove / fall / fleet / flight / flock / galaxy / gang / grove / heap / herd / hive / horde / huddle / jumble / league / library / litter / lock / mass / mob / mound / multitude / pack / pair / panel / peal / pile / range / regiment / series / set / sheaf / shoal / shower / stack / string / swarm / throng / troop / volley / wad

******

205. GROW -- (meaning) to increase in number, size, strength or quality
Synonyms for 'Grow' --
amplify / cultivate / develop / distend / engorge / enlarge / expand / inflate / raise / swell

******

206. GUILTLESS -- (meaning) the fact that somebody has not done anything illegal
Synonyms for 'Guiltless' --
innocent / blameless

******

English Synonyms -- H

207. HARDSHIP -- (meaning) extremely unpleasant situation

Synonyms for 'Hardship' --

difficulty / adversity / misfortune

******

208. HAIRY -- (meaning) covered with a lot of hair

Synonyms for 'Hairy' --

downy / hirsute / furred / furry

******

209. HALLUCINATION -- (meaning) an experience that involves the perception of things that are not present

Synonyms for 'Hallucination' --

apparition / delirium / delusion / illusion / mirage / phantasm

******

210. HALO -- a circle of light around somebody

Synonyms for 'Halo' --

aura / corona / nimbus / radiance

******

211. HAZY -- unclear; dull

Synonyms for 'Hazy' --

foggy / misty / murky

******

212. HEAVY -- weighing a lot

Synonyms for 'Heavy' --

bulky / burdensome / cumbersome / hefty / weighty

******

213. HEED -- (meaning) to pay careful attention

Synonyms for 'Heed' --

notice / observe / watch

******

214. HEINOUS -- (meaning) morally very bad

Synonyms for 'Heinous' --

gruesome / monstrous / offensive / outrageous / scandalous

******

215. HERALD -- (meaning) sign or hint for future event

Synonyms for 'Herald' --

augury / foreshadow / harbinger / indication / precursor / prediction / presage / signal / warning

******

216. HERESY -- (meaning) opposite opinion, especially in religious matters

Synonyms for 'Heresy' --

blasphemy / heterodoxy / irreverence / profanation / sacrilege / unorthodoxy

******

217. HESITATE -- (meaning) to be worried about doing or saying something

Synonyms for 'Hesitate' --

dither / falter / waver / vacillate

******

218. HINDER -- (meaning) to prevent from making progress

Synonyms for 'Hinder' --

block / deter / encumber / forbid / hamper / impede / inhibit / obstruct / prohibit / restrict

******

219. HORRIFYING -- (meaning) causing great fear or shock

Synonyms for 'Horrifying' --

creepy / dreaded / eerie / foreboding / freighting / horrific / horrible / horrendous / panicky / scary / spooky / terrifying

******

220. HOSTILITY -- (meaning) a strong feeling of dislike, disagreement or anger

Synonyms for 'Hostility' --

acrimony / aggression / animosity / antagonism / antipathy / aversion / conflict / contention / enmity / loathing / malevolence / malice / opposition / rancor / resentment / rivalry / spite / strife

******

221. HYGIENE -- (meaning) – an act of keeping yourself and your place clean

Synonyms for 'Hygiene' --

cleanliness / purity /sanitation

******

222. HYPOCRISY -- (meaning) double standard

Synonyms for 'Hypocrisy' --

duplicity / insincerity / pretense

******

English Synonyms -- I

223. IDENTICAL -- (meaning) similar or almost similar

Synonyms for 'Identical' --

alike / equal / matching

******

224. IMMERSE -- (meaning) to put something into a liquid

Synonyms for 'Immerse' --

dip / drench / dunk / engross / marinate / plunge / soak

******

225. IMPLEMENT -- (meaning) to carry out something

Synonyms for 'Implement' --

enforce / execute / perform

******

226. IMPOVERISHED -- (meaning) not having basic things necessary for life

Synonyms for 'Impoverished' --

destitute / needy / poor

******

227. IMPRESSIVE -- (meaning) extremely good

Synonyms for 'Impressive' --

august / awesome / awe-inspiring

******

228. IMPRUDENT -- (meaning) not sensible or wise

Synonyms for 'Imprudent' --

foolish / immature / indiscreet / injudicious / irresponsible / rash / reckless / thoughtless / unconsidered / unwise

******

229. IMPUDENT -- (meaning) very brave and confident

Synonyms for 'Impudent' --

audacious / bold / daring

******

230. INACCURACY -- (meaning) the fact of something being not correct or exact

Synonyms for 'Inaccuracy' --

ambiguity / approximation / elusiveness / erroneousness / estimation / faultiness / imprecision / incorrectness / inexactness / mistakenness / vagueness

******

231. INAPPROPRIATE -- (meaning) not suitable or relevant, etc.

Synonyms for 'Inappropriate' --

extraneous / improper / irrelevant / unconnected / unessential / unsuitable / unrelated

******

232. INCARCERATE -- (meaning) to put somebody in prison

Synonyms for 'Incarcerate' --

arrest / capture / confine / detain / imprison / intern / jail

******

233. INCESSANTLY -- (meaning) never stopping

Synonyms for 'Incessantly' --

ceaselessly / constantly / continually / continuously / endlessly / eternally / interminably / relentlessly / unremittingly

******

234. INDEPENDENCE -- (meaning) freedom to live

Synonyms for 'Independence' --
autonomy / liberty / sovereignty

******

235. INDIFFERENT -- (meaning) having no interest in somebody/something
Synonyms for 'Indifferent' --
blasé / carefree / detached / easygoing / nonchalant / lackadaisical / unconcerned / undaunted

******

236. INEXORABLE -- (meaning) that cannot be changed or stopped
Synonyms for 'Inexorable' --
inevitable / relentless / unalterable / unchangeable / unrelenting / unstoppable

******

237. INFINITE -- (meaning) that cannot be measured
Synonyms for 'Infinite' --
countless / endless / illimitable / immeasurable / incalculable / inestimable / innumerable / limitless / numerous / unfathomable / unlimited / unmeasured

******

238. INSANE -- (meaning) unable to behave in the normal way
Synonyms for 'Insane' --
crazy / deranged / mad

******

239. INSTINCTIVE -- (meaning) done or happening naturally
Synonyms for 'Instinctive' --
automatic / natural / spontaneous

******

240. INTERLOPER -- (meaning) a person who is present somewhere illegally or without permission

Synonyms for 'Interloper' --

gatecrasher / intruder / trespasser

******

241. INTOLERABLE -- (meaning) too bad or difficult to bear

Synonyms for 'Intolerable --

excruciating / insufferable / unbearable / unendurable / unspeakable

******

242. INVIGORATING -- (meaning) making you feel full of energy

Synonyms for 'Invigorating' --

bracing / energizing / fortifying / refreshing / revitalizing / reviving

******

243. IRRESOLUTION -- (meaning) inability to decide what to do

Synonyms for 'Irresolution' --

capriciousness / fickleness / indecisiveness / unpredictability / vacillation / volatility / wavering

******

244. IRRITATE -- (meaning) to cause trouble for somebody

Synonyms for 'Irritate' --

annoy / bother / exasperate

******

245. ISSUE -- (meaning) a thing that is difficult to deal with

Synonyms for 'Issue' --

matter / problem / crisis

******

English Synonyms -- J

246. JAILED -- (meaning) the fact of somebody being in jail

Synonyms for 'Jailed' --

caged / confined / enslaved / fettered / imprisoned / restrained / shackled

******

247. JAGGED -- (meaning) rough, sharp and pointed

Synonyms for 'Jagged' --

bristly / pointed / pointy / prickly / ragged / serrated / spiny / thorny / toothed

******

248. JANGLE -- (meaning) sound of two metals hitting each other

Synonyms for 'Jangle' --

clank / clink / ding / jingle / ping / ring / tinkle

******

249. JARGON -- (meaning) tough words used by particular people

Synonyms for 'Jargon' --

argot / gobbledygook / lingo

******

250. JAUNT -- (meaning) a short and pleasing journey

Synonyms for 'Jaunt' --

excursion / expedition / junket / outing / trip

******

251. JEER -- (meaning) to make an impolite remark to show your dislike

Synonyms for 'Jeer' --

boo / heckle / ridicule / taunt

******

252. JEOPARDIZE -- (meaning) to put somebody in a situation of danger

Synonyms for 'Jeopardize' --

endanger / expose / imperil

******

253. JERK -- (meaning) making sudden short sharp movement

Synonyms for 'Jerk' --

pull / tug / tweak / twitch / wrench / yank

******

254. JITTERY -- (meaning) anxious or nervous

Synonyms for 'Jittery' --

angst / frantic / fretful / grumbling / manic / nervy / panic / vexed

******

255. JUSTICE -- (meaning) fair treatment

Synonyms for 'Justice' --

correctness / equability / equanimity / equity / evenhandedness / honesty / impartiality / integrity / judiciousness / justness / legality / legitimacy / level-headedness / morality / neutrality / prudence / rationality / reasonableness / rectitude / righteousness / sensibleness / truthfulness

******

256. JUSTIFICATION -- (meaning) explanation for something that has happened

Synonyms for 'Justification' --

explanation / rationalization / validation

******

English Synonyms -- K

257. KILLING -- (meaning) an act of ending somebody's life

Synonyms for ***'Killing'*** *--*

annihilation / bloodbath / bloodshed / carnage / execution / massacre / murder / pogrom / slaughter

******

258. KINDLINESS -- (meaning) the quality of being kind and caring

Synonyms for ***'Kindliness'*** *--*

benevolence / bounteousness / compassion / empathy / generosity / gentleness / humanity / kindheartedness / kindness / largesse / liberality / munificence / openhandedness / philanthropy / sensitivity / sympathy / thoughtfulness

******

259. KNOWLEDGE -- (meaning) information, skills and understanding

Synonyms for ***'Knowledge'*** *--*

awareness / erudition / experience / familiarity / know-how / learning / literacy

******

260. KOWTOW -- (meaning) to treat somebody with too much respect to get their favor

Synonyms for ***'Kowtow'*** *--*

crawl / fawn / flatter / grovel / ingratiate / obsequious / smarmy / toady

******

English Synonyms -- L

261. LABEL -- (meaning) small piece of paper, etc. attached to something to give information about it

Synonyms for 'Label' --

stamp / sticker / tag

******

262. LAGGARD -- (meaning) lazy person, authority, etc

Synonyms for 'Laggard' --

dawdler / lazybones / shirker / slacker / slowcoach / straggler

******

263. LAMENT -- (meaning) to feel sorry about something

Synonyms for 'Lament' --

atone / regret / repent

******

264. LAMPOON -- (meaning) to make fun of somebody/something

Synonyms for 'Lampoon' --

burlesque / deride / disdain / mock / ridicule / satirize / scoff / scorn / skit / spoof

******

265. LANDSCAPE -- (meaning) everything that you can see of a large area

Synonyms for 'Landscape' --

countryside / panorama / scene / scenery / topography / vista

******

266. LANE -- (meaning) a narrow road

Synonyms for 'Lane' --

alley / avenue / corridor / path / road / street / track

******

267. LAUGH -- (meaning) to express your happiness through sounds of your face

Synonyms for 'Laugh' --

cackle / chortle / chuckle / gentle / giggle / guffaw / snicker / snigger / titter

******

268. LAUGHABLE -- (meaning) not worth taking seriously

Synonyms for 'Laughable' --

absurd / asinine / ludicrous / mediocre / nonsensical / preposterous / ridiculous / senseless

******

269. LEAN -- (meaning) a person, etc. without much flesh

Synonyms for 'Lean' --

bony / lanky / scrawny / skeletal / skinny / slim / thin / wiry

******

270. LETHAL -- (meaning) harmful and able to cause death

Synonyms for 'Lethal' --

deadly / fatal / mortal

******

271. LIAISE -- (meaning) to act as a cooperative link between two or more groups

Synonyms for 'Liaise' --

adjudicate / arbitrate / coordinate / intercede / mediate / reconcile / settle

******

272. LOFT -- (meaning) room at the top of the house

Synonyms for ‘Loft’ --

attic / garret

******

273. LOCATION -- (meaning) a particular area, position or point

Synonyms for ‘Location’ --

locality / region / site / spot / vicinity / zone

******

274. LOGICAL -- (meaning) based on practical aspects

Synonyms for ‘Logical’ --

commonsensical / rational / sensible

******

275. LOITER -- (meaning) to stand or wait somewhere

Synonyms for ‘Loiter’ --

linger / loaf / lurk / skulk

******

276. LONE -- (meaning) without any other people

Synonyms for ‘Lone’ --

alone / friendless / introverted / solitary / unaccompanied

******

277. LOOK -- (meaning) to see in a particular direction in a particular way

Synonyms for ‘Look’ --

gape / gawk / gaze / glance / glare / glimpse / glower / peek / peep / peer / scowl / sight / spot / squint / stare / watch

******

278. LOQUACIOUS -- (meaning) talking a lot

Synonyms for ‘Loquacious’ --

chatty / **effusive** / **garrulous** / **rambling** / **talkative** / **verbose** / **voluble** / **wordy**

******

279. LOVE -- (meaning) strong feeling of liking

Synonyms for **'Love' --**

adore / **affection** / **fondness** / **warmth**

******

English Synonyms -- M

280. MAGNIFICENT -- (meaning) extremely good

Synonyms for 'Magnificent' --

majestic / royal / splendid

******

281. MALIGN -- (meaning) to say bad things about somebody; to criticize

Synonyms for 'Malign' --

berate / besmirch / defame / denigrate / disparage / libel / revile / slander / sully / taint / tarnish / vilify

******

282. MANDATORY -- (meaning) required by law

Synonyms for 'Mandatory' --

binding / compulsory / enforced / obligatory / requisite / unavoidable

******

283. MEADOW -- (meaning) land covered with grass

Synonyms for 'Meadow' --

field / ground / lawn / pasture / turf

******

284. MELT -- (meaning) to make something become liquid because of heating

Synonyms for 'Melt' --

defrost / liquefy / thaw / unfreeze

******

285. MESSILY -- (meaning) very badly

Synonyms for 'Messily' --

inconsiderately / shoddily / sloppily

******

286. MIGRANT -- (meaning) a person who moves from one place to another

Synonyms for **'Migrant'** --

drifter / **emigrant** / **expatriate** / **hobo** / **immigrant** / **nomad** / **refugee** / **traveler** / **vagabond** / **vagrant** / **wanderer**

******

287. MINDFUL -- (meaning) knowing or realizing something

Synonyms for **'Mindful'** --

aware / **conscious** / **cognizant**

******

288. MISCELLANEOUS -- (meaning) comprising many things that are disconnected from each other

Synonyms for **'Miscellaneous'** --

assorted / **diverse** / **mixed** / **motley** / **sundry** / **varied** / **various**

******

289. MISGIVING -- (meaning) feeling of doubt

Synonyms for **'Misgiving'** --

disbelief / **qualm** / **suspicion**

******

290. MISHAP -- (meaning) an event in which a vehicle hit something causing damage

Synonyms for **'Mishap'** --

accident / **collision** / **crash**

******

291. MISSIVE -- (meaning) official letter

Synonyms for **'Missive'** --

communiqué / dispatch / epistle / memo / memorandum

******

292. MISTRUST -- (meaning) lack of confidence

Synonyms for 'Mistrust' --

distrust / doubt / suspicion

******

293. MOCK -- (meaning) to show no respect; to make fun of somebody

Synonyms for 'Mock' --

belittle / condescend / contempt / criticize / deign / deride / despise / disdain / disparage / disregard / disrespect / humiliate / loathe / ridicule / scoff / scorn / spurn / vilify

******

294. MOISTEN -- (meaning) to make something wet

Synonyms for 'Moisten' --

dampen / drench / humidify / soak / wet

******

295. MOLLYCODDLE -- (meaning) to give too much protection to somebody

Synonyms for 'Mollycoddle' --

cocoon / cosset / overprotect / pamper

******

296. MOLLIFY -- (meaning) to calm down

Synonyms for 'Mollify' --

appease / conciliate / pacify / placate / reconcile / relieve / soothe

******

297. MORASS -- (meaning) an area of soft wet ground

Synonyms for 'Morass' --

bayou / fen / marsh / morass / quagmire / swamp / wetlands

******

298. MORATORIUM -- (meaning) official suspension of an activity

Synonyms for 'Moratorium' --

cessation / halt / pause / standstill / termination

******

299. MOVE -- (meaning) to go somewhere

Synonyms for 'Move' --

accelerate / bolt / bound / breeze / budge / chase / clamber / clamp / crawl / creep / dart / dash / dawdle / fling / follow / gallop / glide / hasten / hike / hobble / hurtle / hurry / inch / jog / limp / lag / lope / lumber / march / meander / mosey / ride / run / parade / poke / plod / prance / race / roam / rove / rush / sashay / scamper / scramble / scoot / scurry / scuttle / shamble / shuffle / skedaddle / skid / slew / slide / slink / slip / slither / slog / sprint / stalk / stamp / stir / stomp / streak / stride / strut / swagger / sway / toddle / trail / traipse / tramp / travel / trek / trip / trot / trudge / trundle / waddle / wade / wander / whiz / whisk / wobble / zoom

******

300. MUSHY -- (meaning) soft to crush or squeeze

Synonyms for 'Mushy' --

mushy / pulpy / spongy / springy / squashy / squishy

******

301. MUTUALLY -- (meaning) done equally by two or more people

Synonyms for 'Mutually' --

collectively / communally / cooperatively / jointly / reciprocally

******

302. MYRIAD -- (meaning) extremely large number of something

Synonyms for **'Myriad'** --

countless / **incalculable** / **innumerable** / **multitude** / **numberless** / **numerous**

******

303. MYSTERIOUS -- (meaning) too strange to be understood

Synonyms for **'Mysterious'** --

enigmatic / **inexplicable** / **mystifying** / **puzzling** / **uncanny** / **unexplained** / **unfathomable**

******

English Synonyms -- N

304. NATIVE -- (meaning) connected with your original living place

Synonyms for **'Native'** --

aboriginal / indigenous / inhabitant / local / natal / national

******

305. NAUGHTY -- (meaning) enjoying playing tricks on others

Synonyms for **'Naughty'** --

impish / playful / prankish / puckish / roguish / waggish / wicked

******

306. NECESSITY -- (meaning) the need for something

Synonyms for **'Necessity'** --

coercion / compulsion / duty / emergency / essential / exigency / obligation / requirement / requisite / urgency

******

307. NEGLIGENT -- (meaning) not giving enough care or attention to somebody/something

Synonyms for **'Negligent'** --

inattentive / slack / slipshod

******

308. NERVOUSLY -- (meaning) thinking about unpleasant things and feeling unhappy and afraid

Synonyms for **'Nervously'** --

agitatedly / anxiously / apprehensively / awfully / dreadfully / edgily / fearfully / fretfully / fussily / intolerably / restlessly / uncomfortably / uneasily / worriedly

******

309. NEVER-ENDING -- (meaning) never coming to an end

Synonyms for **'Never-ending'** --

ceaseless / enduring / eternal / everlasting / lifelong / undying / unending

******

310. NEVERTHELESS -- (meaning) despite the fact that
Synonyms for 'Nevertheless' --
although / but / however / moreover / nonetheless / still / though / yet

******

311. NIL -- (meaning) nothing
Synonyms for 'Nil' --
zero / zilch / zip

******

312. NOISILY -- (meaning) making disturbing or unpleasant noise
Synonyms for 'Noisily' --
deafeningly / loudly / piercingly / raucously / shrilly / stridently / vociferously

******

313. NOTORIOUS -- (meaning) well known for being bad
Synonyms for 'Notorious' --
disreputable / infamous / villainous

******

314. NOVICE -- (meaning) new and with little experience
Synonyms for 'Novice' --
amateur / apprentice / trainee

******

315. NUMBING -- (meaning) making you feel almost nothing
Synonyms for 'Numbing' --
deadening / freezing / sedating

******

English Synonyms -- O

316. OBEDIENCE -- (meaning) the practice of obeying rules, etc.

Synonyms for **'Obedience'** --

adherence / compliance / deference

******

317. OBTAIN -- (meaning) to get something

Synonyms **– access / acquire / gain / receive**

******

318. OCCUPIED -- (meaning) to keep doing something

Synonyms for **'Occupied'** --

active / busy / engaged

******

319. OCCUR -- (meaning) to take place as a result of something

Synonyms for **'Occur'** --

emerge / happen / materialize / surface / transpire

******

320. OFFEND -- (meaning) to displease somebody with your comment

Synonyms for **'Offend'** --

affront / outrage / upset

******

321. OLD -- (meaning) not new or young

Synonyms for **'Old'** --

aged / ancient / antiquated / decrepit / elderly / immemorial / mature / obsolete / bygone / outdated / outmoded / long-established

******

322. OMEN -- (meaning) a feeling that something bad or unpleasant is going to happen or that something unpleasant is true

Synonyms for **'Omen'** --

foreboding / **forewarning** / **hunch** / **inkling** / **intuition** / **menace** / **portent** / **premonition** / **presage** / **presentiment** / **sinister**

******

323. OPPOSE -- (meaning) to express your disagreement
Synonyms for **'Oppose'** --
challenge / **combat** / **contest** / **counter** / **counteract** / **resist**

******

324. ONWARD -- (meaning) towards the front position
Synonyms for **'Onward'** --
advance / **ahead** / **forward**

******

325. OSTRACIZE -- (meaning) to get rid of somebody; to keep out somebody from your group
Synonyms for **'Ostracize'** --
banish / **deport** / **eliminate** / **eschew** / **exclude** / **purge** / **repel** / **repulse** / **shirk** / **shun** / **snub** / **spurn**

******

326. OVERDUE -- (meaning) not done, paid, etc. in return by the expected time
Synonyms for **'Overdue'** --
unpaid / **unsettled**

******

327. OVERLOOK -- (meaning) to not notice or consider something
Synonyms for **'Overlook'** --
condone / **discount** / **dismiss** / **disregard** / **ignore** / **neglect**

******

English Synonyms -- P

328. PAINKILLING -- (meaning) causing you to feel no pain
Synonyms for ‘Painkilling’ --
analgesic / anesthetic / palliative / sedating / tranquilizing

******

329. PAIR -- (meaning) two people or things
Synonyms for ‘Pair’ --
couple / duet / duo

******

330. PALE -- (meaning) [of complexion, etc.] almost white | not dark
Synonyms for ‘Pale’ --
ashen / ashy / colorless / drab / dull / monochrome / pale / pasty / whitish

******

331. PALPABLE -- (meaning) that can be easily noticed
Synonyms for ‘Palpable’ --
apparent / blatant / evident / explicit / flagrant / manifest / noticeable / overt / patent / prominent / unconcealed

******

332. PALTRY -- (meaning) too small in amount or significance
Synonyms for ‘Paltry’ --
insignificant / measly / miserable / petty / slight / trifling / trivial / worthless

******

333. PART -- (meaning) a piece or characteristic of something
Synonyms for ‘Part’ --
fraction / fragment / portion / section / segment / slice

******

334. PARTITION -- (meaning) to split something into two or more parts

Synonyms for ***'Partition'*** --

Synonyms – **divide** / **separate** / **segregate**

******

335. PASTIME -- (meaning) an activity that somebody does for enjoyment

Synonyms for ***'Pastime'*** --

leisure / **pursuit** / **recreation**

******

336. PEACEFUL -- (meaning) calm; not disturbed

Synonyms for ***'Peaceful'*** --

composed / **halcyon** / **placid** / **restful** / **serene** / **still** / **tranquil** / **unperturbed** / **unruffled**

******

337. PERILOUS -- (meaning) very dangerous

Synonyms for ***'Perilous'*** --

hazardous / **precarious** / **treacherous**

******

338. PERMEATE -- (meaning) to spread in all directions

Synonyms for ***'Permeate'*** --

diffuse / **disseminate** / **pervade**

******

339. PERPETUAL -- (meaning) never coming to an end

Synonyms for ***'Perpetual'*** --

eternal / **everlasting** / **unending**

******

340. PERSISTENT -- continuing uninterruptedly

Synonyms for ***'Persistent'*** --

constant / **continual** / **importunate** / **pushy** / **relentless**

******

341. PERSUADE -- (meaning) to make somebody do something through argument or reasoning

*Synonyms for **'Persuade'** --*

convince / **induce** / **influence**

******

342. PHLEGMATIC -- (meaning) lazy

*Synonyms for **'Phlegmatic'** --*

indolent / **slothful** / **sluggish**

******

343. PINNACLE -- (meaning) the highest or most successful part of something

*Synonyms for **'Pinnacle'** --*

acme / **apex** / **climax** / **peak** / **summit** / **tip** / **zenith**

******

344. PLAUSIBLE -- (meaning) reasonable explanation

*Synonyms for **'Plausible'** --*

believable / **conceivable** / **convincing** / **credible** / **incontrovertible** / **infallible** / **undoubted** / **pragmatic** / **rational** / **realistic** / **reliable** / **unquestionable**

******

345. PLEAD -- (meaning) to ask somebody for something

*Synonyms for **'Plead'** --*

beg / **beseech** / **entreat** / **implore** / **importune** / **seek** / **solicit**

******

346. PLENTIFUL -- (meaning) available in large numbers or amount

*Synonyms for **'Plentiful'** --*

abound / **ample** / **abundant** / **sufficient**

******

347. POSIT -- (meaning) to make an opinion in order to use it as a basis of a theory, etc.

Synonyms for ***'Posit'*** *--*

conceive / conjecture / hypothesize / postulate / speculate

******

348. PRECISE -- (meaning) very true or obvious

Synonyms for ***'Precise'*** *--*

accurate / clear / exact

******

349. PREDILECTION -- (meaning) extreme liking towards something

Synonyms for ***'Predilection'*** *--*

fondness / inclination / preference / proclivity / propensity / tendency

******

350. PREJUDICE -- (meaning) an unreasonable strong feeling in favor of or against somebody; preferential treatment

Synonyms for ***'Prejudice'*** *--*

bias / discrimination / favoritism / inclination / inequality / injustice / nepotism / partiality / preconception / predisposition / unfairness / wrongness

******

351. PREVALENT -- (meaning) very common

Synonyms for ***'Prevalent'*** *--*

ever-present / ubiquitous / widespread

******

352. PROCLAIM -- (meaning) to say something publicly and officially; to announce

Synonyms for ***'Proclaim'*** *--*

broadcast / decree / pronounce / publicize / transmit

******

353. PRODIGIOUS -- (meaning) extremely large or powerful
Synonyms for 'Prodigious' --
colossal / formidable / phenomenal / staggering / unparalleled

******

354. PRODUCE -- (meaning) to make something
Synonyms for 'Produce' --
build / compose / construct / create / fabricate / invent / manufacture / originate

******

355. PROFLIGATE -- (meaning) using money, etc. in a careless way
Synonyms for 'Profligate' --
extravagant / improvident / luxurious / overgenerous / spendthrift / squanderer / uneconomical / wasteful

******

356. PROGRESS -- (meaning) to make improvement in something
Synonyms for 'Progress' --
advance / develop / growth / proceed

******

357. PROMPT -- (meaning) the quality of being fast
Synonyms for 'Prompt' --
abrupt / brisk / direct / hasty / hurried / immediate / instant / nippy / quick / rapid / speedy / sudden / swift

******

358. PROPOSAL -- (meaning) important idea or plan to do the best thing
Synonyms for 'Proposal' --
offer / recommendation / scheme / suggestion

******

359. PROSPER -- (meaning) to be successful
Synonyms for 'Prosper' --

flourish / grow / thrive

******

360. PROSPEROUS -- (meaning) having a lot of money
Synonyms for 'Prosperous' --
affluent / flush / lavish / lush / luxurious / moneyed / opulent / rich / sumptuous / wealthy / well-off

******

361. PROVOKE -- (meaning) to do something to cause a particular reaction
Synonyms for 'Provoke' --
goad / incite / prod

******

362. PUFF -- (meaning) to breathe loudly or noisily
Synonyms for 'Puff --
gasp / huff / pant / sulk / wheeze

******

363. PUNTER -- (meaning) user or buyer of a product or service
Synonyms for 'Punter' --
client / consumer / customer / payer / procurer / purchaser / shopper / spender

******

364. PURSUE -- (meaning) to follow
Synonyms for 'Pursue' --
chase / ensue / track / trail

******

English Synonyms -- Q

365. QUANDARY -- (meaning) unpleasant and difficult situation where you have to make a particular choice

Synonyms for 'Quandary' --

dilemma / fix / predicament

******

366. QUASH -- (meaning) to cancel the legal decision

Synonyms for 'Quash' --

abolish / abrogate / annul / invalid / invalidate / negate / nullify / overturn / repeal / rescind / retract / revoke / terminate / void / withdraw

******

367. QUIETUDE -- (meaning) the state of being still, calm and quiet

Synonyms for 'Quietude' --

composed / composure / equanimity / hushed / peace / poised / silence / tranquility / unflustered / unmoved / unruffled

******

English Synonyms -- R

368. RAGE -- (meaning) feeling of uncontrollable anger
Synonyms for 'Rage' --
bile / ferocity / frenzy / fury / ire / rage / temper / wrath

******

369. RAMSHACKLE -- (meaning) broken down; disorganized
Synonyms for 'Ramshackle' --
decrepit / derelict / dilapidated / rickety / tumbledown

******

370. RANSACK -- (meaning) to search in an untidy way
Synonyms for 'Ransack' --
raid / comb / scour

******

371. RAUCOUS -- (meaning) making a lot of noise; noisy
Synonyms for 'Raucous' --
deafening / earsplitting / piercing / rowdy / shrill

******

372. REBELLION -- (meaning) disobedience to or opposition of authority
Synonyms for 'Rebellion' --
defiance / insurgence / insurrection / mutiny / rebellion / recalcitrance / revolt / sedition / subversion / uprising

******

373. RECEDE -- (meaning) to decrease or withdraw
Synonyms for 'Recede' --
ebb / fade / recoil / retreat

******

374. RECENT -- (meaning) of the present time
Synonyms for 'Recent' --

current / modern / latest

******

375. RECLAIM -- (meaning) to get something back
Synonyms for 'Reclaim' --
recapture / recoup / recover / regain / repossess / retrieve

******

376. RECLINE -- (meaning) to sit or lie down in order to relax
Synonyms for 'Recline' --
bask / laze / loll / lounge / slouch / slump / sprawl

******

377. REFUSE -- (meaning) to say 'no'
Synonyms for 'Refuse' --
decline / deny / disprove / rebuff / refute / reject

******

378. REGION -- (meaning) a place with particular features
Synonyms for 'Region' --
area / vicinity / zone

******

379. REIMBURSEMENT -- (meaning) money paid for damages suffered
Synonyms for 'Reimbursement' --
compensation / damages / reparation

******

380. REITERATE -- (meaning) to repeat
Synonyms for 'Reiterate' --
recap / recapitulate / regurgitate / rehearse

******

381. REJOICE -- (meaning) to enjoy something special
Synonyms for 'Rejoice' --

celebrate / party / revel

******

382. RELEASE -- (meaning) to come out
Synonyms for 'Release' --
discharge / emanate / emit / exude / hold / originate / produce / radiate / secrete

******

383. RELUCTANCE -- (meaning) not wanting to do something
Synonyms for 'Reluctance' --
apathy / disinclination / indifference / unwillingness

******

384. RELEGATE -- (meaning) to move somebody/something down to a lower level
Synonyms for 'Relegate' --
demote / devalue / downgrade

******

385. RELOCATE -- (meaning) to move somebody from one place to another
Synonyms for 'Relocate' --
reposition / shuffle / transfer

******

386. REMNANT -- (meaning) the remaining parts of something
Synonyms for 'Remnant' --
leftover / remainder / remains / residue / scrap / vestige

******

387. REPHRASE -- (meaning) to say or write something using different words
Synonyms for 'Rephrase' --
paraphrase / rearticulate / redraft / restate / retell / reword / rewrite

******

388. REPLICA -- (meaning) a thing that is the same as something else
Synonyms for **'Replica'** --
copy / **duplicate** / **facsimile**

******

389. REPLY -- (meaning) to give a reaction
Synonyms for **'Reply'** --
answer / **react** / **respond**

******

390. RIPOSTE -- (meaning) quick reply to a criticism
Synonyms for **'Riposte'** --
comeback / **counter** / **rejoinder** / **retort**

******

391. REPROVE -- (meaning) to not approve somebody's actions, to criticize
Synonyms for **'Reprove'** --
admonish / **chastise** / **chide** / **condemn** / **rebuke** / **reprimand** / **reproach** / **reproof** / **scold**

******

392. RESIGN -- (meaning) to leave your job or organization officially
Synonyms for **'Resign'** --
abandon / **abdicate** / **quit** / **relinquish** / **renounce**

******

393. RESPECT -- (meaning) feeling of admiration
Synonyms for **'Respect'** --
deference / **regard** / **reverence**

******

394. RESTRAIN -- (meaning) to forcefully stop somebody from doing something

Synonyms for *'Restrain'* --

bridle / circumscribe / constrain / constrict / contain / control / limit / suppress

******

395. RETALIATION -- (meaning) settling of scores
Synonyms for *'Retaliation'* --
reprisal / retribution / revenge / vengeance

******

396. REVIVE -- (meaning) to be conscious, healthy, and strong again
Synonyms for *'Revive'* --
rejuvenate / restore / resurrect / revitalize

******

397. REVOLVE -- (meaning) to move around a central fixed point
Synonyms for *'Revolve'* --
gyrate / pivot / roll / rotate / spin / swivel

******

398. RIPPLE -- (meaning) to move like a wave
Synonyms for *'Ripple'* --
heave / ripple / roll / undulate

******

399. ROUTINE -- (meaning) a fixed way of performing actions
Synonyms for *'Routine'* --
customary / habitual / regular

******

400. RULE -- (meaning) to manage and control the affairs of a country, etc.
Synonyms for *'Rule '* --
administer / direct / govern / oversee / regulate / superintend / supervise
******

English Synonyms -- S

401. SACRED -- (meaning) treated with great respect

Synonyms for 'Sacred' --

blessed / deified / hallowed / holy / revered / sanctified

******

402. SATISFIED -- (meaning) having got what you wanted

Synonyms for 'Satisfied' --

complacent / content / fulfilled / pleased

******

403. SCARCE -- (meaning) available in very small quantities

Synonyms for 'Scarce' --

inadequate / insufficient / lacking / meager / negligible / rare / scant / scanty / wanting

******

404. SCHOLASTIC -- (meaning) connected with education

Synonyms for 'Scholastic' --

academic / educational / scholarly

******

405. SCRATCH -- (meaning) a cut, mark, etc.

Synonyms for 'Scratch' --

abrasion / scrape / scuff

******

406. SCRUTINIZE -- (meaning) to consider a subject or an idea carefully

Synonyms for 'Scrutinize' --

analyze / check / evaluate / examine / inspect / monitor / observe / study

******

407. SEIZE -- (meaning) to take illegal goods away from somebody

Synonyms for 'Seize' --

capture / confiscate / impound / snatch

******

408. SENTIMENTAL -- (meaning) showing too much emotion

Synonyms for 'Sentimental' --

gushy / mawkish / mushy / overemotional / sappy / schmaltzy / slushy / syrupy

******

409. SHORTEN -- (meaning) to make something short

Synonyms for 'Shorten' --

abridge / abbreviate / edit

******

410. SIGNIFICANT -- (meaning) very important

Synonyms for 'Significant' --

considerable / critical / essential / indispensable / necessary / substantial / vital

******

411. SLAY -- (meaning) to kill somebody

Synonyms for 'Slay' --

assassinate / eliminate / execute

******

412. SMASH -- (meaning) to break something into many pieces; to crush

Synonyms for 'Smash' --

crumble / crunch / drudge / grind / macerate / mince / pound / pulverize

******

413. SMILE -- (meaning) an expression of happiness on the face

Synonyms for 'Smile' --

beam / grin / gummy / simper / smirk / sneer

******

414. SNOBBISH -- (meaning) too proud

Synonyms for 'Snobbish' --

arrogant / bigheaded / conceited / haughty / scornful / supercilious

******

415. SOOTHING -- (meaning) to make somebody feel less angry by doing a favor to them

Synonyms for 'Soothing --

appeasing / conciliate / placatory

******

416. SOUR -- (meaning) strong and unpleasant sweet

Synonyms for 'Sour' --

acerb / acrid / bitter

******

417. SPARKLING -- (meaning) shining and flashing with light; bright

Synonyms for 'Sparkling' --

dazzling / glassy / gleaming / glinting / glistening / glittery / glossy / glowing / incandescent / luminescent / luminous / lustrous / polished / radiant / reflecting / shimmering / shining / shiny / sparkling / sparkly

******

418. SPOIL -- (meaning) to damage something badly

Synonyms for 'Spoil' --

besmirch / blemish / blight / deface / defile / despoil / devastate / disfigure / mar / mutilate / ruin / sabotage / scar / slander / sully / taint / tarnish / vandalize / vilify / wreck

******

419. SPRUCE -- (meaning) neat and clean

Synonyms for 'Spruce' --

dapper / elegant / stylish / well-dressed / well-groomed

******

420. SQUASH -- (meaning) to press something firmly

Synonyms for 'Squash' --

mash / pulp / puree / squeeze

******

421. STONY -- having a lot of stones

Synonyms for 'Stony' --

flinty / gravelly / gritty / pebbly / rocky / shingly

******

422. STRAND -- a single thin piece of something

Synonyms for 'Strand' --

fiber / filament / string / thread / tress / wisp

******

423. STRIP -- a long and narrow piece of cloth, paper, etc.

Synonyms for 'Strip' --

band / ribbon / shred / stripe

******

424. STELLAR -- (meaning) connected with stars

Synonyms for 'Stellar' --

astral / astronomical / astrophysical / cosmological / solar

******

425. STOCK -- (meaning) a supply of something that is available for use

Synonyms for 'Stock' --

hoard / reserve / stash / stockpile / store

******

426. STORY -- (meaning) description of events

Synonyms for 'Story' --

allegory / anecdote / chronicle / fable / journal / legend / log / memoir / narrative / parable / tale / yarn

******

427. STRATEGY -- the particular method to achieve your aim

Synonyms for 'Strategy' --

approach / plan / policy / stratagem / tactic

******

428. SUBJUGATE -- (meaning) to gain control over something

Synonyms for 'Subjugate' --

beat / conquer / defeat / overcome / overpower / subdue / suppress / surmount / trounce / vanquish

******

429. SUBSIDE -- (meaning) to become less strong

Synonyms for 'Subside' --

abate / decline / decrease

******

430. SUBSTANCE -- (meaning) a type of solid, liquid or gas

Synonyms for 'Substance' --

material / matter / stuff

******

431. SUBVERSIVE -- (meaning) destructing the political system

Synonyms for 'Subversive' --

defiant / dissenting / mutinous / rebellious / seditious

******

432. SUCCESSION -- (meaning) several people, things, events, etc. of a similar type that follows each other

Synonyms for 'Succession' --

chain / cycle / progression / sequence / series / string

******

433. SUPPLEMENTARY -- (meaning) provided in addition to something else

Synonyms for 'Supplementary' --

additional / ancillary / auxiliary / secondary / subsidiary

******

434. STIMULATE -- (meaning) to make somebody/something more active

Synonyms for 'Stimulate' --

motivate / rouse / stir

******

435. STRINGENT -- (meaning) very strict

Synonyms for 'Stringent' --

harsh / severe / stern / strict

******

436. SUCCINCT -- (meaning) having a short description

Synonyms for 'Succinct' --

brief / concise / laconic / summarizing / pithy

******

437. SUFFERING -- (meaning) mental or physical pain

Synonyms for *'Suffering'* --

affliction / agony / anguish / dejection / distress / grief / hardship / misery / ordeal / sadness / torment / torture / woe

******

438. SUFFOCATE -- (meaning) to prevent somebody from taking breath

Synonyms for *'Suffocate'* --

asphyxiate / choke / smother / strangle / stifle / throttle

******

439. SUGARY -- (meaning) containing sugar

Synonyms for *'Sugary'* --

sugared / sweetened / syrupy

******

440. SULK -- (meaning) to be very quiet and impolite to show your anger

Synonyms for *'Sulk'* --

brood / languish / mope / pine / pout

******

441. SUMMARY -- (meaning) main points of a book, report, etc.

Synonyms for *'Summary'* --

abridgment / abstract / digest / outline / review / synopsis

******

442. SUPERB -- (meaning) of very high quality

Synonyms for *'Superb'* --

awesome / brilliant / charismatic / excellent / fabulous / fantastic / glorious / grand / magnificent / marvelous / outstanding / spectacular / splendid / tremendous / wonderful

******

443. SUPERSEDE -- (meaning) to replace by somebody/something better

Synonyms for **'Supersede' --**

exceed / succeed / supplant / surpass

******

444. SURE -- (meaning) having no doubts

Synonyms for **'Sure' --**

certain / confident / definite

******

445. SURPLUS -- (meaning) more than is necessary

Synonyms for **'Surplus' --**

excess / glut / oversupply / surfeit

******

446. SURPRISED -- (meaning) showing a feeling caused by something (pleasant or unpleasant) suddenly or unexpectedly

Synonyms for **'Surprised' --**

amazed / aghast / appalled / astonished / astounded / dazed / dumbfounded / flabbergasted / horrified / shaken / shocked / staggered / startled / stunned / thunderstruck

******

English Synonyms -- T

447. TACKLE -- (meaning) to deal with the difficult situation

Synonyms for 'Tackle' --

face / confront / undertake

******

448. TANGIBLE -- (meaning) that can be touched

Synonyms for 'Tangible' --

corporeal / physical / touchable

******

449. TANGY -- (meaning) strong sharp taste or smell

Synonyms for 'Tangy' --

aromatic / flavorful / peppery / piquant / pungent / savory / spicy

******

450. TEMPEST -- (meaning) violent storm

Synonyms for 'Tempest' --

blizzard / gale / hurricane / snowstorm / whiteout

******

451. TENDER -- (meaning) showing feelings of care

Synonyms for 'Tender' --

affectionate / delicate / gentle

******

452. TERMINATE -- (meaning) to come to an end

Synonyms for 'Terminate' --

cease / conclude / finish / stop

******

453. THANKFULNESS -- (meaning) the state of showing your thanks

Synonyms for 'Thankfulness' --

appreciation / gratefulness / gratitude / recognition

******

454. THEORY – a set of ideas that tries to explain a phenomenon, etc.
Synonyms for 'Theory' --
assumption / concept / conjecture / hypothesis / notion / postulation / presumption / presupposition / speculation / supposition

******

455. THREATENING -- (meaning) expressing a threat of harm or violence
Synonyms for 'Threatening' --
baleful / alarming / daunting / looming / malevolent / malicious / malignant / menacing / nasty / spiteful / vindictive / wicked

******

456. THRIFTY -- (meaning) using money, etc. in a careful way
Synonyms for 'Thrifty' --
skimping / stingy / tightfisted / sparing / parsimonious

******

457. THOROUGHLY-- (meaning) completely
Synonyms for 'Thoroughly' --
broadly / comprehensively / expansively / extensively / largely / lengthily / widely

******

458. TIMID -- (meaning) not willing to do difficult things; nervous about meeting other people
Synonyms for 'Timid' --
bashful / cowardly / craven / fearful / frightened / gutless / hesitant / nervous / panicky / pusillanimous / scared / shy / spineless / timorous

******

459. TORPID -- (meaning) slow to notice things; not active
Synonyms for 'Torpid' --

apathetic / dozy / drowsy / enervated / inactive / indolent / languorous / lazy / lethargic / listless / nodding / relaxed / sleepy / sluggish / somnolent / unenergetic

******

460. TRADITIONAL -- (meaning) following older methods
Synonyms for 'Traditional' --
conventional / customary / habitual

******

461. TRANSMIT -- (meaning) to send a message from one person to another
Synonyms for 'Transmit' --
broadcast / communicate / convey

******

462. TRASH -- (meaning) items that are no longer needed
Synonyms for 'Trash' --
debris / garbage / junk / litter / rubbish / rubble / scrap / wreckage

******

463. TRAINED -- (meaning) a person with special knowledge
Synonyms for 'Trained' --
expert / professional / proficient / skilled / specialized

******

464. TREMBLE -- (meaning) to make a slight movement
Synonyms for 'Tremble' --
quiver / shake / shiver / shudder / vibrate / wobble

******

465. TRIVIAL -- (meaning) not important
Synonyms for 'Trivial' --
insignificant / nominal / titular

******

English Synonyms -- U

466. ULTIMATELY -- (meaning) in the end

Synonyms for 'Ultimately' --

eventually / finally / lastly

******

467. UNACCUSTOMED -- (meaning) not usual or familiar

Synonyms for 'Unaccustomed' --

impracticable / uncommon / unfamiliar / unfeasible / unworkable

******

468. UNAPOLOGETIC -- (meaning) not sorry

Synonyms for 'Unapologetic' --

impenitent / unabashed / unapologetic / unreformed / unremorseful / unrepentant

******

469. UNAVOIDABLE -- (meaning) that cannot be avoided, prevented or ignored

Synonyms for 'Unavoidable' --

inescapable / inevitable / inexorable / unpreventable

******

470. UNBECOMING -- (meaning) not appropriate or suiting

Synonyms for 'Unbecoming' --

unappealing / unbefitting / uncomplimentary / unflattering / ungainly / unsuitable

******

471. UNBRIDLED -- not controlled or restricted

Synonyms for 'Unbridled' --

rampant / unchecked / unconstrained / uncontrolled / unhindered / uninhibited / unrestrained

******

472. UNCERTAIN -- (meaning) not sure

*Synonyms for **'Uncertain'** --*

doubtful / dubious / debatable / disputed / incredulous / suspicious / unconvinced / questionable

******

473. UNCONTAMINATED -- (meaning) not spoilt by harmful things

*Synonyms for **'Uncontaminated'** --*

antibacterial / antiseptic / sterilized / unadulterated / unpolluted / untainted

******

474. UNEQUIVOCAL -- (meaning) that has clear meaning

*Synonyms for **'Unequivocal'** --*

categorical / definite / explicit / incontestable / incontrovertible / indisputable / indubitable / irrefutable / unambiguous / unarguable / unmistakable / unquestionable

******

475. UNFLAGGING -- (meaning) tireless

*Synonyms for **'Unflagging'** --*

indefatigable / tireless / unfaltering / untiring

******

476. UNFOLD -- (meaning) to make something begin

*Synonyms for **'Unfold'** --*

commence / initiate / originate

******

477. UNITY -- (meaning) working together in agreement

Synonyms for 'Unity' --

accord / amity / camaraderie / concord / friendship / harmony / solidarity

******

478. UNOFFICIAL -- (meaning) not following strict rules

Synonyms for 'Unofficial' --

casual / informal / unauthorized

******

479. UNUSUAL -- (meaning) different from what is normal

Synonyms for 'Unusual' --

anomalous / atypical / bizarre / eccentric / odd / outlandish / peculiar / uncanny / weird

******

480. URGENT -- (meaning) something that is very important to do

Synonyms for 'Urgent' --

crucial / imperative / vital

******

English Synonyms -- V

481. VALIDATE -- (meaning) to prove that something is true

Synonyms for 'Validate' --

attest / authenticate / certify / corroborate / endorse / substantiate / verify

******

482. VANISH -- (meaning) to disappear suddenly or in an inexplicable way

Synonyms for 'Vanish' --

diminish / evaporate / fade / wane

******

483. VENOMOUS -- (meaning) containing poison

Synonyms for 'Venomous' --

noxious / poisonous / toxic

******

484. VIBRANT -- (meaning) full of life and energy

Synonyms for 'Vibrant' --

animated / boisterous / bouncy / bubbly / chirpy / dynamic / effervescent / energetic / lively / playful / spirited / vigorous / vivacious

******

English Synonyms -- W

485. WALK -- (meaning) to move or go somewhere but not running
Synonyms for 'Walk' --
amble / clump / creep / dawdle / lumber / march / meander / mooch / mosey / plod / potter / promenade / prowl / ramble / roam / saunter / skulk / slog / stalk / stride / stroll / trail / traipse / tramp / tread / trudge / wander

******

486. WARLIKE -- (meaning) ready to fight
Synonyms for 'Warlike' --
combative / confrontational / belligerent

******

487. WATCHFUL -- (meaning) very careful
Synonyms for 'Watchful' --
cautious / heedful / observant / vigilant

******

488. WELD -- (meaning) to join
Synonyms for 'Weld' --
bind / fuse / solder

******

489. WET -- (meaning) containing water or other liquid
Synonyms for 'Wet' --
awash / clammy / damp / humid / juicy / luscious / moist / soaked / soggy / succulent

******

490. WHINE -- (meaning) to complain in an annoying way
Synonyms for 'Whine' --
bellyache / bemoan / gripe / grouse / grumble / moan / nag

******

491. WISDOM -- (meaning) ability to make sensible and good decisions

Synonyms for 'Wisdom' --

acuity / acumen / acuteness / aptitude / brainpower / comprehension / discernment / discretion / enlightenment / expertise / insight / insightfulness / intellect / intelligence / judgment / judiciousness / perceptiveness / prudence / sharpness / smartness / understanding

******

492. WIT -- (meaning) amusing talks

Synonyms for 'Wit' --

chitchat / comedy / drollness / humor / repartee

******

493. WIZENED -- (meaning) smaller with many folds or lines

Synonyms for 'Wizened' --

crinkly / crumple / shriveled / shrunken / wrinkled

******

494. WONDER -- (meaning) to be very surprised

Synonyms for 'Wonder' --

amaze / astonish / astound / marvel / stun

******

495. WORRY -- (meaning) to keep thinking about unpleasant things

Synonyms for 'Worry' --

angst / anxiety / apprehension / care / concern / trouble

******

496. WRECK -- (meaning) to completely destroy something

Synonyms for 'Wreck' --

devastate / ravage / raze / ruin

******

English Synonyms -- XYZ

497. YANK -- (meaning) to quickly and suddenly pull something

Synonyms for 'Yank' --

drag / draw / haul / heave / jerk / jolt / lug / tow / tug

******

498. YARDSTICK -- (meaning) a standard to judge or compare how good or successful something is

Synonyms for 'Yardstick' --

benchmark / gauge / index / level / measure / scale / standard

******

499. YELL -- (meaning) to shout or cry loudly

Synonyms for 'Yell' --

bawl / bellow / blub / blubber / growl / holler / howl / roar / scream / screech / shriek / snivel / squeal / wail / whimper / yelp / yowl

******

500. YUMMY -- (meaning) [of food] very good to eat

Synonyms for 'Yummy' --

delectable / delicious / luscious / mouthwatering / palatable / scrumptious / tasty

******

501. ZEALOT -- (meaning) strong supporter

Synonyms for 'Zealot' --

adherent / admirer / aficionado / enthusiast / fan / follower / supporter / backer / zealous

****

About the Author

Manik Joshi was born on January 26, 1979, at Ranikhet, a picturesque town in the Kumaon region of the Indian state of Uttarakhand. He is a permanent resident of the Sheeshmahal area of Kathgodam located in the city of Haldwani in the Kumaon region of Uttarakhand in India. He completed his schooling in four different schools. He is a science graduate in the ZBC – zoology, botany, and chemistry – subjects. He is also an MBA with a specialization in marketing. Additionally, he holds diplomas in "computer applications", "multimedia and web-designing", and "computer hardware and networking". During his schooldays, he wanted to enter the field of medical science; however, after graduation, he shifted his focus to the field of management. After obtaining his MBA, he enrolled in a computer education center; he became so fascinated with working on the computer that he decided to develop his career in this field. Over the following years, he worked at some computer-related full-time jobs. Following that, he became interested in Internet Marketing, particularly in domaining (business of buying and selling domain names), web design (creating websites), and various other online jobs. However, later he shifted his focus solely to self-publishing. Manik is a nature-lover. He has always been fascinated by overcast skies. He is passionate about traveling and enjoys solo travel most of the time rather than traveling in groups. He is actually quite a loner who prefers to do his own thing. He likes to listen to music, particularly when he is working on the computer. Reading and writing are definitely his favorite pastimes, but he has no interest in sports. Manik has always dreamed of a prosperous life and prefers to live a life of luxury. He has a keen interest in politics because he believes it is politics that decides everything else. He feels a sense of gratification sharing his experiences and knowledge with the outside world. However, he is an introvert by nature and thus gives prominence to only a few people in his personal life. He is not a spiritual man, yet he actively seeks knowledge about the metaphysical world; he is particularly interested in learning about life beyond death. In addition to writing academic/informational text and fictional content, he also maintains a personal diary. He has always had a desire to stand out from the crowd. He does not believe in treading the beaten path and avoids copying someone else's path to success. Two things he always refrains from are smoking and drinking; he is a teetotaler and very health-conscious. He usually wakes up before the sun rises. He starts his morning with meditation and exercise. Fitness is an integral and indispensable part of his life. He gets energized by solving complex problems. He loves himself the way he is and he loves the way he looks. He doesn't believe in following fashion trends. He dresses according to what suits him & what he is comfortable in. He believes in taking calculated risks. His philosophy is to expect the best but prepare for the worst. According to him, you can't succeed if you are unwilling to fail. For Manik, life is about learning from mistakes and figuring out how to move forward.

Amazon Author Page of Manik Joshi:
https://www.amazon.com/author/manikjoshi
Email: manik85joshi@gmail.com

BIBLIOGRAPHY

(A). SERIES TITLE: "ENGLISH DAILY USE" *[40 BOOKS]*

01. How to Start a Sentence
02. English Interrogative Sentences
03. English Imperative Sentences
04. Negative Forms In English
05. Learn English Exclamations
06. English Causative Sentences
07. English Conditional Sentences
08. Creating Long Sentences In English
09. How to Use Numbers In Conversation
10. Making Comparisons In English
11. Examples of English Correlatives
12. Interchange of Active and Passive Voice
13. Repetition of Words
14. Remarks In the English Language
15. Using Tenses In English
16. English Grammar- Am, Is, Are, Was, Were
17. English Grammar- Do, Does, Did
18. English Grammar- Have, Has, Had
19. English Grammar- Be and Have
20. English Modal Auxiliary Verbs
21. Direct and Indirect Speech
22. Get- Popular English Verb
23. Ending Sentences with Prepositions
24. Popular Sentences In English
25. Common English Sentences
26. Daily Use English Sentences
27. Speak English Sentences Everyday
28. Popular English Idioms and Phrases
29. Common English Phrases
30. Daily English- Important Notes
31. Collocations In the English Language
32. Words That Act as Multiple Parts of Speech (Part 1)
33. Words That Act as Multiple Parts of Speech (Part 2)
34. Nouns In the English Language
35. Regular and Irregular Verbs
36. Transitive and Intransitive Verbs

37. 10,000 Useful Adjectives In English
38. 4,000 Useful Adverbs In English
39. 20 Categories of Transitional Expressions
40. How to End a Sentence

****

(B). SERIES TITLE: "ENGLISH WORD POWER" *[30 BOOKS]*

01. Dictionary of English Synonyms
02. Dictionary of English Antonyms
03. Homonyms, Homophones and Homographs
04. Dictionary of English Capitonyms
05. Dictionary of Prefixes and Suffixes
06. Dictionary of Combining Forms
07. Dictionary of Literary Words
08. Dictionary of Old-fashioned Words
09. Dictionary of Humorous Words
10. Compound Words In English
11. Dictionary of Informal Words
12. Dictionary of Category Words
13. Dictionary of One-word Substitution
14. Hypernyms and Hyponyms
15. Holonyms and Meronyms
16. Oronym Words In English
17. Dictionary of Root Words
18. Dictionary of English Idioms
19. Dictionary of Phrasal Verbs
20. Dictionary of Difficult Words
21. Dictionary of Verbs
22. Dictionary of Adjectives
23. Dictionary of Adverbs
24. Dictionary of Formal Words
25. Dictionary of Technical Words
26. Dictionary of Foreign Words
27. Dictionary of Approving & Disapproving Words
28. Dictionary of Slang Words
29. Advanced English Phrases
30. Words In the English Language

****

(C). SERIES TITLE: "WORDS IN COMMON USAGE" [10 BOOKS]

01. How to Use the Word "Break" In English
02. How to Use the Word "Come" In English
03. How to Use the Word "Go" In English
04. How to Use the Word "Have" In English
05. How to Use the Word "Make" In English
06. How to Use the Word "Put" In English
07. How to Use the Word "Run" In English
08. How to Use the Word "Set" In English
09. How to Use the Word "Take" In English
10. How to Use the Word "Turn" In English

****

(D). SERIES TITLE: "WORDS BY NUMBER OF LETTERS" [10 BOOKS]

01. Dictionary of 4-Letter Words
02. Dictionary of 5-Letter Words
03. Dictionary of 6-Letter Words
04. Dictionary of 7-Letter Words
05. Dictionary of 8-Letter Words
06. Dictionary of 9-Letter Words
07. Dictionary of 10-Letter Words
08. Dictionary of 11-Letter Words
09. Dictionary of 12- to 14-Letter Words
10. Dictionary of 15- to 18-Letter Words

****

(E). SERIES TITLE: "ENGLISH WORKSHEETS" [10 BOOKS]

01. English Word Exercises (Part 1)
02. English Word Exercises (Part 2)
03. English Word Exercises (Part 3)
04. English Sentence Exercises (Part 1)
05. English Sentence Exercises (Part 2)
06. English Sentence Exercises (Part 3)
07. Test Your English
08. Match the Two Parts of the Words
09. Letter-Order In Words
10. Choose the Correct Spelling

Made in the USA
Monee, IL
09 January 2023

24846731R00056